W9-AGF-578

Pronouns

Kelly Doudna

Published by SandCastle™, an imprint of ABDO Publishing Company, 4940 Viking Drive, Edina, Minnesota 55435.

Printed in the United States.

Photo credits: Comstock, Digital Stock, Eyewire Images, Image 100, Rubber Ball

Library of Congress Cataloging-in-Publication Data

Doudna, Kelly, 1963-
    Pronouns / Kelly Doudna.
      p. cm. -- (Sentences)
    Includes index.
    ISBN 1-57765-619-9
     1. English language--Pronoun--Juvenile literature. [1. English language--Pronoun.] I. Title.

PE1261 .D68 2001
428.2--dc21

2001022893

The SandCastle concept, content, and reading method have been reviewed and approved by a national advisory board including literacy specialists, librarians, elementary school teachers, early childhood education professionals, and parents.

Let Us Know

After reading the book, SandCastle would like you to tell us your stories about reading. What is your favorite page? Was there something hard that you needed help with? Share the ups and downs of learning to read. We want to hear from you! To get posted on the Abdo Publishing Company Web site, send us email at:

sandcastle@abdopub.com

About SandCastle™
Nonfiction books for the beginning reader

- Basic concepts of phonics are incorporated with integrated language methods of reading instruction. Most words are short, and phrases, letter sounds, and word sounds are repeated.

- Readability is determined by the number of words in each sentence, the number of characters in each word, and word lists based on curriculum frameworks.

- Full-color photography reinforces word meanings and concepts.

- "Words I Can Read" list at the end of each book teaches basic elements of grammar, helps the reader recognize the words in the text, and builds vocabulary.

- Reading levels are indicated by the number of flags on the castle.

Look for more SandCastle books
in these three reading levels:

Level 1 (one flag)	**Level 2** (two flags)	**Level 3** (three flags)

Grades Pre-K to K 5 or fewer words per page	**Grades K to 1** 5 to 10 words per page	**Grades 1 to 2** 10 to 15 words per page

Pronouns

A pronoun is a word that replaces a noun.

Pronouns

My dad teaches me how to swing at a baseball.

Pronouns

My sister and I bake cookies.

They will taste good.

Pronouns

I have three apples.

They are red.

Pronouns

We are fishing.

We did not catch anything yet.

Pronouns

I like my ice cream cone.

It tastes sweet.

Pronouns

I cannot believe what I just heard.

Pronouns

I sit with Mom.

She reads a story to me.

Pronouns

Who are my friends?

(them or they)

21

Words I Can Read

Nouns

A noun is a person, place, or thing

baseball
  (BAYSS-bawl) p. 7
dad (DAD) p. 7
ice cream cone (EYESS
  kreem kohn) p. 15
noun (NOUN) p. 5

pronoun
  (PROH-noun) p. 5
sister (SISS-TUR) p. 9
story (STOR-ee) p. 19
word (WURD) p. 5

Plural Nouns

A plural noun is more than one
person, place, or thing

apples (AP-uhlz) p. 9
cookies (KUK-eez) p. 9

friends (FRENDZ) p. 21

Verbs
A verb is an action or being word

are (AR) pp. 11, 13, 21
bake (BAYK) p. 9
believe (bi-LEEV) p. 17
cannot (KAN-not) p. 17
catch (KACH) p. 13
did (DID) p. 13
fishing (FISH-ing) p. 13
have (HAV) p. 11
heard (HURD) p. 17
is (IZ) p. 5

like (LIKE) p. 15
reads (REEDZ) p. 19
replaces (ri-PLAYSS-ez) p. 5
sit (SIT) p. 19
swing (SWING) p. 7
taste (TAYST) p. 9
tastes (TAYSTSS) p. 15
teaches (TEECH-iz) p. 7
will (WILL) p. 9

Adjectives
An adjective describes something

good (GUD) p. 9
my (MYE) pp. 7, 9, 15, 21
red (RED) p. 11

sweet (SWEET) p. 15
three (THREE) p. 11

Match each picture to the
pronoun that replaces the noun

he

it

she

they